by Iain Gray

WRITING *to* REMEMBER

WRITING *to* REMEMBER

79 Main Street, Newtongrange,
Midlothian EH22 4NA
Tel: 0131 344 0414   Fax: 0845 075 6085
E-mail: info@lang-syne.co.uk
www.langsyneshop.co.uk

Design by Dorothy Meikle
Printed by Ricoh Print Scotland
© Lang Syne Publishers Ltd 2012

ISBN 978-1-85217-227-5

Gray

Echoes of a far distant past
can still be found in most names

Chapter one:

Origins of Scottish surnames

by George Forbes

It all began with the Normans.

For it was they who introduced surnames into common usage more than a thousand years ago, initially based on the title of their estates, local villages and chateaux in France to distinguish and identify these landholdings, usually acquired at the point of a bloodstained sword.

Such grand descriptions also helped enhance the prestige of these arrogant warlords and generally glorify their lofty positions high above the humble serfs slaving away below in the pecking order who only had single names, often with Biblical connotations as in Pierre and Jacques.

The only descriptive distinctions among this peasantry concerned their occupations, like Pierre the swineherd or Jacques the ferryman.

The Normans themselves were originally Vikings (or Northmen) who raided, colonised and eventually settled down around the French coastline.

They had sailed up the Seine in their long-boats in 900AD under their ferocious leader Rollo and ruled the roost in north east France before sailing over to conquer England, bringing their relatively new tradition of having surnames with them.

It took another hundred years for the Normans to percolate northwards and surnames did not begin to appear in Scotland until the thirteenth century.

These adventurous knights brought an aura of chivalry with them and it was said no damsel of any distinction would marry a man unless he had at least two names.

The family names included that of Scotland's great hero Robert De Brus and his compatriots were warriors from families like the De Morevils, De Umphravils, De Berkelais, De Quincis, De Viponts and De Vaux.

As the knights settled the boundaries of

their vast estates, they took territorial names, as in Hamilton, Moray, Crawford, Cunningham, Dunbar, Ross, Wemyss, Dundas, Galloway, Renfrew, Greenhill, Hazelwood, Sandylands and Church-hill.

Other names, though not with any obvious geographical or topographical features, nevertheless derived from ancient parishes like Douglas, Forbes, Dalyell and Guthrie.

Other surnames were coined in connection with occupations, castles or legendary deeds. Stuart originated in the word steward, a prestigious post which was an integral part of any large medieval household. The same applied to Cooks, Chamberlains, Constables and Porters.

Borders towns and forts – needed in areas like the Debateable Lands which were constantly fought over by feuding local families – had their own distinctive names; and it was often from them that the resident groups took their communal titles, as in the Grahams of Annandale, the Elliots and Armstrongs of the East Marches, the Scotts and Kerrs of Teviotdale and Eskdale.

Even physical attributes crept into surnames, as in Small, Little and More (the latter being 'beg' in Gaelic), Long or Lang, Stark, Stout, Strong or Strang and even Jolly.

Mieklejohns would have had the strength of several men, while Littlejohn was named after the legendary sidekick of Robin Hood.

Colours got into the act with Black, White, Grey, Brown and Green (Red developed into Reid, Ruddy or Ruddiman). Blue was rare and nobody ever wanted to be associated with yellow.

Pompous worthies took the name Wiseman, Goodman and Goodall.

Words intimating the sons of leading figures were soon affiliated into the language as in Johnson, Adamson, Richardson and Thomson, while the Norman equivalent of Fitz (from the French-Latin 'filius' meaning 'son') cropped up in Fitzmaurice and Fitzgerald.

The prefix 'Mac' was 'son of' in Gaelic and clans often originated with occupations – as in MacNab being sons of the Abbot, MacPherson and MacVicar being sons of the minister and MacIntosh being sons of the chief.

The church's influence could be found in the names Kirk, Clerk, Clarke, Bishop, Friar and Monk. Proctor came from a church official, Singer and Sangster from choristers, Gilchrist and Gillies from Christ's servant, Mitchell, Gilmory and Gilmour from servants of St Michael and Mary, Malcolm from a servant of Columba and Gillespie from a bishop's servant.

The rudimentary medical profession was represented by Barber (a trade which also once included dentistry and surgery) as well as Leech or Leitch.

Businessmen produced Merchants, Mercers, Monypennies, Chapmans, Sellers and Scales, while down at the old village watermill the names that cropped up included Miller, Walker and Fuller.

Other self explanatory trades included Coopers, Brands, Barkers, Tanners, Skinners, Brewsters and Brewers, Tailors, Saddlers, Wrights, Cartwrights, Smiths, Harpers, Joiners, Sawyers, Masons and Plumbers.

Even the scenery was utilised as in Craig, Moor, Hill, Glen, Wood and Forrest.

Rank, whether high or low, took its place with Laird, Barron, Knight, Tennant, Farmer, Husband, Granger, Grieve, Shepherd, Shearer and Fletcher.

The hunt and the chase supplied Hunter, Falconer, Fowler, Fox, Forrester, Archer and Spearman.

The renowned medieval historian Froissart, who eulogised about the romantic deeds of chivalry (and who condemned Scotland as being a poverty stricken wasteland), once sniffily dismissed the peasantry of his native France as the jacquerie (or the jacques-without-names) but it was these same humble folk who ended up overthrowing the arrogant aristocracy.

In the olden days, only the blueblooded knights of antiquity were entitled to full, proper names, both Christian and surnames, but with the passing of time and a more egalitarian, less feudal atmosphere, more respectful and worthy titles spread throughout the populace as a whole.

Echoes of a far distant past can still be found in most names and they can be borne with pride in commemoration of past generations who fought and toiled in some capacity or other to make our nation what it now is, for good or ill.

Chapter two:

Battle honours

There are three possible sources for the origin of the surname of Gray, or Grey, including that it may have been simply a descriptive term to denote someone's hair colouring, complexion, or clothing.

But the exploits of those who have borne it over the centuries are certainly more colourful than the name may suggest.

Another explanation is that it originates from a Norman known as Fulbert, who held the powerful post of Great Chamberlain to Robert, Duke of Normandy, who granted him the lands known as Croy, in the French region of Picardy.

'Croy' is thought to have derived from the French 'Les Payes de Croix', meaning 'The Lands of the Cross', and Fulbert later adopted de Croy ('of Croy') as the family surname and it is his daughter, Arlette, or Herleva, who was the mother of William the Conqueror, victor of the battle of Hastings in 1066.

The name Croy then took on various forms, including Groy, Grai, Gray, and Grey.

A John de Grai, for example, is recorded as having been born in Picardy in 1033.

Those de Croys who settled in England in the wake of the Conquest later adopted the form of Grey (with an 'e'), and their descendants included the ill-starred Lady Jane Grey, the great grand-daughter of Henry VII who was pro-claimed Queen Regent of England for nine days in 1553 – but was deposed and later executed.

The most common spelling of the name is Gray (with an 'a'), and a John de Gray, a descendant of Lord Grey of Chillingham, in Northumberland, is recorded in Coldstream, in the Scottish Borders, during the reign from 1249 to 1286 of Alexander III, while a Hugo de Gray is recorded in Fife earlier in the same century.

The third possible source of the name is from the Scottish Gaelic 'glas', or 'glass', denoting

the colour gray, and from this derives the
Highland names of Glas, Glass, and MacGlashan.

In the decades following the abortive
Jacobite Rising of 1745 and the subsequent
enforced depopulation of the Highlands and
Islands, many MacGlashans were forced to seek
a new home in the Lowlands, where many later
adopted the anglicised form of 'Gray'.

A family of Grays were the hereditary
sheriffs of Forfarshire, responsible for building
both Broughty Castle and Castle Huntly, while
separate families of Grays established in the
Lowlands held lands in Ayrshire and the lands of
Carntyne, east of the present day city of
Glasgow.

Both the numerous Lowland families of
Grays and their MacGlashan counterparts in the
Highlands fought bravely in the cause of
Scotland's freedom and independence, while
many also took arms in defence of the cause of
the Royal House of Stuart.

Foremost among these Scottish patriots
was Sir Andrew Gray, who played a prominent

role in the bitter and bloody Wars of Independence with England.

It had been in 1292 that John Balliol was controversially enthroned at Scone as King of Scots – but, fatefully for the nation, it had been the Scots themselves who had unwisely asked the powerful Edward I of England to arbitrate in the bitter dispute over the succession to the throne, and the hapless Balliol had found himself Edward's chosen man.

Scotland rose in revolt against the imperialist designs of Edward in July of 1296 but, living up to his sobriquet of 'Hammer of the Scots', the ruthless monarch brought the entire nation under his subjugation little less than a month later, garrisoning strategic locations throughout the length and breadth of the nation.

Rubbing salt into the stinging wounds of Scottish pride, 1,500 earls, bishops, and burgesses, were forced to sign a humiliating treaty of fealty to the rapacious Edward.

Among those who had no option but to sign the treaty, known as the Ragman Roll because of the profusions of ribbons that dangle from the seals of the signatories, was Sir Andrew Gray.

The humiliation was soon to be avenged, however, when William Wallace raised the banner of revolt against the English occupation of Scotland in May of 1297.

Proving an expert in the tactics of guerrilla warfare, Wallace and his hardened band of freedom fighters inflicted stunning defeats on the English garrisons.

This culminated in the liberation of practically all of Scotland following the battle of Stirling Bridge, on September 11, 1297.

Defeat followed at the battle of Falkirk on July 22, 1298, however, and Wallace was eventually betrayed and captured in August of 1305.

On August 23 of that year, he was brutally executed in London on the orders of a vengeful Edward I.

Less than a year later, the banner of revolt against the mailed fist of English occupation was raised yet again following the enthronement at Scone of Robert the Bruce as King of Scots.

One of the great warrior king's ablest supporters was Sir Andrew Gray, who played a key role in March of 1314 in ousting the English garrison from the mighty bastion of Edinburgh Castle in a daring night raid.

Sir Andrew, along with the Earl of Moray and about thirty of their hardy men, made a precarious ascent by rope ladder up the forbidding north face of the rock on which the castle is perched, while another force prepared to launch an assault on the castle's south gate.

Sir Andrew was among the first to clamber over the castle walls and the signal was then given for the assault on the south gate.

A furious struggle ensued with the garrison, but it was eventually taken, to the glory of both Sir Andrew Gray and the Earl of Moray.

The capture of the castle was a significant strategic coup, and this was followed up less than three months later with what proved to be the final nail in the coffin of England's imperialist designs on Scotland.

This was the battle of Bannockburn,

fought in June of 1314, and which involved the crushing and humiliating defeat of a 20,000-strong English army under Edward II by a Scots army less than half this strength.

By midsummer of a year earlier an English garrison under the command of Sir Philip Mowbray occupied the imposing fortress of Stirling Castle.

Bruce's brother, Edward, rashly agreed to a pledge by Mowbray that if the castle was not relieved by battle by midsummer of the following year, then he would surrender.

This made battle inevitable, and by June 23 of 1314 the two armies faced one another at Bannockburn, in sight of the castle.

It was on this day that Bruce slew the English knight Sir Henry de Bohun in single combat, but the battle proper was not fought until the following day, shortly after the rise of the midsummer sun.

The English cavalry launched a desperate but futile charge on the densely packed ranks of Scottish spearmen known as schiltrons, and by the time the sun had sank slowly in the west the English army had been totally routed, with Edward himself only narrowly managing to make his escape from the carnage of the battlefield.

Bruce later rewarded Sir Andrew with the grant of lands that included Longforgen, in Perthshire, while the family's honours were added to in 1444 when one of his descendants, also Sir Andrew Gray, was created Lord Gray by James II.

Chapter three:

Murder and intrigue

**The 1st Lord Gray's successors continued to
play a role at the heart of Scotland's frequent-
ly turbulent affairs, with Patrick, the Master
of Gray, son of the 2nd Lord Gray, holding the
influential position of Gentleman of the
Bedchamber to James II.**

It was in this role, as a close companion
and confidante of the king, that he became
involved in one of the darkest incidents of the
king's reign – the murder in 1452 of William, the
8th Earl of Douglas.

The earl had entered into a bond, or
agreement, of mutual alliance with the equally
powerful nobles the Earl of Ross and the Earl
of Crawford, in which they pledged to work
together for their common interests. Understand-
ably suspicious and alarmed by this, James sum-
moned the earl of Douglas to Stirling Castle and
demanded that he revoke the agreement.

The bold earl haughtily refused and, furious at his royal authority being flouted, the king shouted 'since you will not, I shall!' and, drawing his dagger, stabbed him in the neck and body.

As the earl reeled in shock and pain, the Master of Gray felled him with one vicious sweep of a battleaxe. Lying helpless, the Earl of Douglas was then stabbed a further twenty- six times.

What made the murder all the more heinous was that the earl had been granted a safe conduct pass to Stirling, and his brother, in revenge, later pillaged the town and dragged the pass through the filth of the streets at the tail of a horse.

The 3rd Lord Gray was appointed Lord Justice General of Scotland in 1506, while thirty-six years later, in 1542, the 5th Lord Gray was among the many Scottish nobles captured and later ransomed by the English after the battle of Solway Moss.

Following his release from captivity he later became a staunch adherent of Scotland's religious Reformation and an opponent of Mary,

Queen of Scots, who was forced to abdicate in 1568 in favour of her son, the future James VI.

His descendant Andrew, however, the 8th Lord Gray, became embroiled in the bitter civil war that raged in Scotland between 1638 and 1649.

This war was between the Royalists and those Presbyterian Scots who had signed a National Covenant.

The Covenant opposed the divine right of the Stuart monarchy and Royalists such as James Graham, 1st Marquis of Montrose, whose prime allegiance was to Charles I.

Although Montrose had initially supported the Covenant, his conscience later forced him to switch sides, and the period from 1644 to 1645 became known as the Year of Miracles because of his brilliant military successes, but he was finally defeated at Philiphaugh, near Selkirk, in September of 1645.

Lord Gray was ordered to be banished from Scotland for his support of the Royalist cause.

The sentence was never carried out, however, but he was excommunicated by the General Assembly of the Church of Scotland.

William Gray of Pittendrum was another devoted Royalist and commanded one of Charles II's regiments at the battle of Worcester, fought in September of 1651.

The forces of Oliver Cromwell soundly defeated the Royalists, and the king was forced to flee into exile, while William Gray was killed six years later in a duel.

The fortunes of the Grays in the north of Scotland were closely allied to those of Clan Stewart of Atholl and Clan Sutherland.

Any Grays of today who can trace a descent from the ancient homelands of these clans are accordingly entitled to share in their heritage and traditions and adopt their respective tartans.

There are, however, several Gray coats of arms, crests, and mottos, including the motto of 'Anchor fast anchor' and crest of an anchor.

Grays are also considered a sept, or

branch, of both clans, and the motto of Clan Sutherland is 'Without fear', while its crest is a cat.

Sutherland, south of Caithness in the far north of Scotland, is the homeland from which the Sutherlands took their name, and the Sutherland earldom is claimed to be the oldest in Britain.

One tradition is that the MacGlashan/ Gray link with the clan arose when the son of a laird of Foulis sought refuge in the Sutherland homelands after killing a prominent citizen of Dundee.

'MacGlashan', one of the Scottish Gaelic forms of Gray, was the name of a clan that became attached to the Stewarts of Atholl, with one theory being that they may have acted as property lawyers to this clan whose motto is 'Courage grows strong at a wound', and whose crest is a pelican feeding its young.

There is also a tradition that the link arose when a son of the house of the Stewarts of Ballechin, a branch of the Stewarts of Atholl, changed his name to MacGlashan after a bitter family feud.

As kinsfolk of the Stewarts of Atholl, one of the several branches of the Royal House of Stewart that had its origins in the twelfth century, the MacGlashans/Grays fought for the Jacobite cause during the abortive 1745 Rising.

Prince Charles Edward Stuart had stepped ashore on the small Outer Hebridean island of Eriskay on July 22, 1745, landing on the mainland at Loch nan Uamh three days later.

The Jacobite Standard was raised on August 19, at Glenfinnan, on Loch Shiel.

Victory over the government forces was achieved at the battle of Prestonpans in September, and in October the confident prince and his army set off on the long march south to London to claim what was believed to be the rightful Stuart inheritance of the throne.

The army reached only as far as Derby, however, before the controversial decision was taken in early December to withdraw back over the border.

They were destined to pay a bloody price for their support, however, when Jacobite hopes were dashed forever at the battle of Culloden, fought on Drummossie Moor, near Inverness, on April 16, 1746.

In what was the last major battle fought on British soil, hundreds of clansmen died on the battlefield while hundreds of others died later from their wounds and the brutal treatment of their government captors.

The Atholl Brigade had been in the thick of the fighting at Culloden, posted on the extreme right of the front line, and suffered heavy casualties.

Chapter four:

Invention and acclaim

Far from the carnage of the battlefield, generations of Grays have achieved distinction and fame in a range of pursuits ranging from the sciences and medicine to literature and the stage.

Born in Barnesville, Ohio, in 1835, Elisha Gray, founder of the Western Electric Manufacturing Company in 1872, is considered by some to have invented the telephone in his laboratory in Highland Park, Illinois, before Alexander Graham Bell - although today it is the latter who receives the credit.

In contemporary times, Jim Gray is a distinguished American computer scientist, while 'Gray Code' is a technique used in electromechanics developed in the early 1950s by Frank Gray.

In the world of medicine, Henry Gray was the English surgeon and anatomist famous for the medical textbook *Gray's Anatomy*.

Known as 'the Bible of anatomy', seven editions were published between 1860 and 1880 alone, while a 39th edition was published in 2004.

Considered one of the most popular poems in the English language, *Elegy Written in a Country Churchyard*, or, simply, *Gray's Elegy*, was written by the English poet, classical scholar and history professor Thomas Gray, who was born in London in 1716.

Gray, who died in 1771, is buried in Stoke Poges churchyard, in Buckinghamshire, where he is believed to have written his famous poem.

Zane Grey, born in Zanesville, Ohio, in 1872 and who died in 1939, was the hugely popular author of a series of 'Wild West' novels, including *Riders of the Purple Sage* and *Lone Star Ranger*, which was later adapted as a film in 1930.

Alasdair Gray, born in Riddrie, in the east end of Glasgow in 1934, is the talented Scottish writer and artist whose acclaimed first novel *Lanark*, written over a period of thirty years was first published in 1981.

His 1992 novel *Poor Things* won a Whitbread Book of the Year Award. A former student and lecturer at Glasgow School of Art, Gray also illustrates his own books, in addition to producing his own murals and paintings.

Born in Barrington, Rhode Island, in 1941, Spalding Gray was the American actor, playwright, and screenwriter who was best known for his monologues, one of which formed the basis for the 1987 film *Swimming to Cambodia*.

He was found drowned in New York's East River in 2004, and is believed to have committed suicide following bouts of depression he sustained after receiving severe injuries in a car crash three years earlier.

Muriel Gray, born in East Kilbride in 1959, is the Scottish journalist and broadcaster, whose 1995 first novel *The Trickster* set her on the path to becoming a best-selling writer of horror fiction, and whose work has been praised by that master of the genre himself, Stephen King.

On the stage, Joel Grey, who was born Joel Katz in Cleveland, Ohio, in 1932, and whose father was the comedian and musician Mickey Katz, is the American actor who won an Academy Award as Best Supporting Actor for his role as the Master of Ceremonies in the 1972 film *Cabaret*.

Continuing a family stage tradition his daughter, Jennifer Grey, born in 1960, is the actress best known for her role of Frances 'Baby' Houseman in the 1987 film *Dirty Dancing*, which also starred Patrick Swayze.

In the world of music, David Gray, born in Manchester in 1968, is the singer/songwriter who first achieved international success with his 1999 album *White Ladder*, while Macy Gray, born Natalie McIntyre in Canton, Ohio, in 1970, is the multi-talented soul and rhythm and blues singer, songwriter, actress, and record producer whose film credits include *Training Day* and *Scary Movie 3*.

In the world of sport, Andy Gray, born in Glasgow in 1953, is the former Scottish footballer who now pursues a career as a popular media pundit.

Throughout his highly successful playing career he played for Dundee, Aston Villa, Wolverhampton Wanderers, and latterly Everton, when the team won the 1984 FA Cup and the 1985 League and European Cup Winners' Cup.